Red Land

Yellow River

A Story from the Cultural Revolution

Ange Zhang

GROUNDWOOD BOOKS
HOUSE OF ANANSI PRESS
TORONTO BERKELEY

ONE

In 1966 I was a teenager living with my family in downtown Beijing. Like many Chinese homes, our house was built around a small courtyard, called Square Yard. My parents lived on the north side of the courtyard, my grandparents lived in the west wing, and my younger sister and brother and I lived in the east and south wings. In the center we had a small garden where we grew sunflowers, cucumbers, cabbage and green beans.

We had a good life. My father was a famous writer. He wrote the words for the "Yellow River Cantata," which was sung by Chinese people all over the world. When I was little, my teacher invited my father to my school to talk about his writing. I felt a bit embarrassed, because I never got good marks on my writing assignments.

Still, I could draw, and I was the best in my class. My heroes were the Communist army soldiers. I drew a lot of warriors.

A photograph of my family taken at our home. I am in the middle.

I was very happy at school and in our Square Yard. Then, in June, the Cultural Revolution started, and within weeks my school went through a total change. More and more of my classmates joined the Red Guards, Chairman Mao Zedong's specially chosen troops.

The teachers were driven out of our classrooms. One day, the principal was dragged to the football field in front of the whole school. Half of her hair had been shaved off. The Red Guards poured red ink over her head. All the students surrounded the platform where she was standing and chanted, "Long live the Cultural Revolution! Down with the capitalist pigs!" I shouted these things, too, even though I did not know what they meant.

Life was confusing, but it was also fun and exciting. Instead of learning Chinese and math, we memorized the quotations of our leader, Chairman Mao. After school we would all paste posters and revolutionary slogans in the streets. Soon every alley and street in Beijing was filled with a tide of red paper and people wearing red armbands.

One morning when I arrived at school, I noticed that two huge posters hung on each side of the front gate. One poster read: THE GOOD GUY'S SON IS A HERO. The other poster said: THE BAD GUY'S SON IS A BASTARD. I was proud that my parents were high-ranking officials in the party. They were the good guys.

About two dozen Red Guards stood outside the gate. As each person walked through, we had to declare our family background. Some said their families belonged to the Communist Party or army or that they came from families of workers and peasants. They walked through the gate proudly. Those whose families were landlords and business owners walked past the Red Guards with their heads bent low like criminals.

My father had joined Mao's revolution when he was young. Now it was my turn.

"What's your family background?" one of the guards asked me.

"Communist Party," I answered proudly.

(Top) In 1939, my father was a Red Army officer and had just finished writing the words for the "Yellow River Cantata." He is also in the picture below taken at Yian-an, the Red Army base.

(Right) When I was ten years old I became a Young Pioneer. Teenagers could join the Communist Youth League. The next level of membership was to belong to the Communist Party itself.

My friend Hong was a Red Guard and his parents were senior army officials. His marks in school were not impressive, but he was good at sports. We both played on the school soccer team, and he often came to my house to visit. I envied his olive green uniform and the red band he wore on his left arm. I told Hong that I was applying to be a Red Guard, too.

A few days later Hong called me out of the classroom. His face was very serious. It seemed that someone had objected to my application because my father was a writer.

"Did you know your father is one of the bad guys?" he said in a low voice.

I stared at him, trying to understand what he was saying. My father was a high-ranking official in the Communist Party. He had supported Mao and the Communist Party right from the beginning.

"I knew you wouldn't believe me," he said when he saw my bewildered face. "You'll have to see for yourself. Come to the C.W.A.A. building this afternoon." Then his voice became very serious. "We are in a cruel political struggle. You must decide where you stand."

The C.W.A.A. was the home of the Chinese Writers and Artists Association. My parents had often taken me there to see shows for Chinese New Year. It looked like a palace, surrounded by a wall, with a guard house at the entrance and wide steps leading up to four big columns. Four stories loomed above the colonnade, and there was a beautiful big theater on the second floor. But that afternoon the building no longer looked magnificent. Big posters covered the corridor walls. The air was filled with the smell of newspaper and paste.

The auditorium was packed with students and workers. The meeting had already begun. Angry chanting rumbled in the air as I threaded my way through the crowd and finally found a gap where I could see.

In the center of the stage stood the famous artist, Hua, surrounded by Red Guards. I knew him. His paintings had been admired by millions of Chinese people.

Now there was a big plate like a garbage can lid hanging from his neck. The plate had writing on it proclaiming him to be a bad guy. He also wore a pointed hat made of white cardboard. The guards told him to bow his head down low, but when he did, his tall hat would fall off. Then someone would pick it up and force it back onto his head again.

Several other people lined the sides of the stage. They also had plates on their chests, and their heads were bent low.

Standing among them was my father. He wore gray trousers and a white shirt, the same clothes I had seen him wearing earlier that morning. Up on the stage, he looked thin and frail. He bent his head down. His left arm hung slightly crooked, the result of a fall off a horse when he was in the army.

Suddenly, several Red Guards pushed my father into the center of the stage. A terrifying feeling gripped me.

"Down with the counter-revolutionaries!" one of the guards shouted into the microphone. A sea of arms rose up as thousands of voices repeated the words.

My hand went up, too. But I could not find my voice. I dared not look toward the stage. I kept my head low, wishing I could hide away where no one could see me.

Not long after that, we heard a loud banging on our front gate as we were eating dinner one evening. The maid went to open the gate.

About twenty Red Guards stormed in. Most of them pushed their way into my father's study. One of them was my father's chauffeur, whom we called Uncle Hu. He was wearing a red armband. He told my sister, brother and me to stay in a room with our grandparents.

"Your father is a bad man," he said. "You must draw a line between yourselves and him."

I could hear the noise of things being smashed coming from the study, one loud crash after another. Grandma held us in her arms. Her hands were shaking.

My father had many beautiful things, many antiques. They smashed his Ming vases and antique paintings on the ground of the courtyard and took all of his diaries and manuscripts.

I helped my mother clean up. Buried in the broken china I saw a terra cotta Buddha's head that used to be displayed on the bookshelf. My father had once told me it was very valuable old earthenware from the Han Dynasty. I was never even allowed to touch it.

I picked it up. It was heavy in my hand and, surprisingly, it was not broken. The Buddha's face looked so peaceful. It was smiling.

I was just about to place it carefully on the desk when I heard my father's voice.

"Throw it out," he said. He was sitting at the desk, his hand over his eyes.

I wanted to ask him why, but I said nothing as I dropped the Buddha's head back into the rubbish heap.

My school life changed. Suddenly I was a "black kid," the enemy of the revolution. I no longer asked about joining the Red Guards.

Every day, the black kids were ordered to clean the hallways and washrooms. My old friends like Hong avoided me in the halls and schoolyard. I was not allowed to go to student assemblies or march with the others. Every morning I walked past the sign on the main gate: THE BAD GUY'S SON IS A BASTARD. That was me.

I didn't know why all this was happening, and no one would explain it to me. It seemed that no one knew. I was ashamed and angry. I recited

Chairman Mao's quotations over and over, even though I did not understand much. To show the Red Guards that I was as loyal to Chairman Mao as anyone else, I even changed my name from Ange to Weige, which meant to safeguard the revolution.

All I wanted was to be just like the other kids, to wear the olive green uniform with the red armband.

But things kept happening to remind me that I was not like the others.

Many people collected souvenir badges such as these, showing Mao Zedong.

TWO

Before long, my father was arrested. My mother, who worked at the Traditional Opera Research Institute, was being criticized at her work unit. The Red Guards took over the west wing of our house, the rooms my grandparents had lived in. Our maid was ordered to return to her countryside home. Grandpa became ill and died soon after that. My aunt, a high-school teacher who had moved almost all across China to work for the revolution, committed suicide when her own students became Red Guards and turned on her.

At school, more and more Red Guard groups were formed, each one claiming to be more revolutionary than the rest. They began to fight with each other, which made things easier for us black kids. We were no longer the main targets of the Red Guards.

As I was quite good at drawing and calligraphy, I was often called to make big posters for the Red Guards. Soon my posters were everywhere. But no one asked me to join their organization. I looked at my classmates with their red armbands and was full of envy at their good fortune to have been born into good families.

One afternoon, I walked past a stamp shop downtown. In the shop window I saw many palm-sized stamps bearing the names of various Red Guard organizations. For fifteen cents I could have a stamp made.

The discovery cheered me up. Why couldn't I set up a Red Guard group the way the others did? That very evening, I designed an impressive stamp with the image of Tiananmen in the middle and Chairman Mao's words, "Rebellion is justified," on top. It was red, the color of joy. I named my organization the Beijing Red Star Rebel Corps. I was charged an extra fifteen cents by the shop because of the complexity of my design, but from then on, I, too, was a Red Guard.

The schools were closed, and several months passed. One day, I met my friend Hong in the street. He told me he was going to Guangzhou, a city in southern China, to support a Red Guard group called the Red Flag Corps, which was fighting against another Red Guard organization. Three other boys were going with him, and he invited me to join them. We would all be given free train tickets and travel allowances.

I was extremely flattered. To show my enthusiasm and commitment, I had my head shaved. With my new skin head, I thought I looked just like the other Red Guards.

My mother said nothing when she saw me.

It took three days to get to Guangzhou from Beijing. The train was very crowded. People were wedged into luggage racks and under benches. I listened to Hong and his friends gossiping about the people they knew in the party, the fights that were going on among the various Red Guard organizations. They bragged about how they had ransacked someone's home and beaten them up. They talked as if they had a mission, and I was thrilled to be with them. I forgot all about my family.

Finally, I was joining the revolution.

In Guangzhou, we were sent to the Zhongshan Medical School, which housed a branch of the Red Flag Corps. The building looked like a military camp, with piles of sandbags blockading the main gate and guards with machine guns and steel helmets. Two anti-aircraft guns had been mounted on the soccer field.

Every evening I could hear gunshots. Ambulances rushed to and from the emergency center attached to the medical institute, bringing in more and more injured. We were given handguns and taught how to shoot them. I rode a motorcycle for the first time. Everything was dangerous and exciting.

One evening, the loudspeaker on campus suddenly warned everybody to get ready for a big battle. We were told that the Red Flag Corps had attacked the opposition's headquarters and seized two armored vehicles. Now the rival group was going to launch a counter-attack. They had gathered thousands of people. They were going to attack us that night. We gathered on the soccer field and swore to fight to the death.

None of us had ever experienced anything like this. The group from our dorm was given a hand grenade and a few homemade fire bombs.

That night, the campus became quiet, the buildings lit with huge floodlights that cast shadows on the walls. The time had come for me to

show my true colors. I would not do anything that would bring shame to my friends.

As we waited, I thought about death. I thought of my father and wondered where he was. Strangely, I remembered the Buddha's head that was buried in the rubble after the Red Guards ransacked our home. Why was his smile so peaceful?

Eventually, I fell asleep to the sounds of gun shots.

When I opened my eyes, it was broad daylight. I was extremely happy to discover that I was still alive. The attack had been a false alarm.

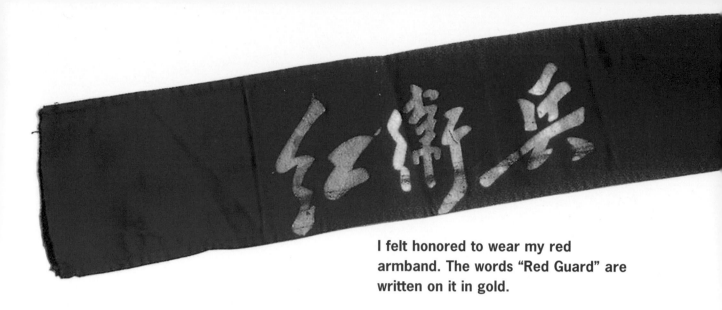

I felt honored to wear my red armband. The words "Red Guard" are written on it in gold.

When I returned home several weeks later, Beijing had changed. The streets were a sea of posters with Mao's words on every wall, bus and train. Shop signs had been smashed. Store windows were filled only with pictures of Mao. The school was almost deserted. Shattered lightbulbs and broken desks and chairs littered the classrooms. There were no teachers; only a few guards patrolling the hallways.

The movie theaters showed the same films every day and radios broadcast the same revolutionary operas. The art gallery only showed exhibitions of peasant art. So we all just hung around on the streets. There was nothing to do.

I began to visit Hong and his friends at their Red Guard office. I was not a member of their organization, but they didn't mind me hanging around. Before long, I found something I could do to help. Answer the telephone.

The telephone was a symbol of privilege. Not many student organizations had one. I was happy to take and deliver messages. It made me feel as if I was part of their revolutionary activities. I knew they had gathered together hundreds of Red Guards to destroy the headquarters of other groups. Hong's group had pasted a huge poster on the entrance of the Ministry of Public Security, criticizing their political opinions.

I was so proud of my friends.

One evening, when I was in Hong's office, a big crowd suddenly broke into the room. They were from a rival Red Guard group, and they were carrying iron bars. Without warning, they started to smash everything in the room.

I immediately thought of hiding the telephone, but it was too late. I was surrounded. A young man in uniform approached me with his hands behind his back.

"Put down the telephone," he ordered.

I stepped back and suddenly felt something metal strike my face. I fell, and as the telephone dropped to the floor, somebody smashed it with an iron bar. My eyes were blind, but I felt that black telephone breaking into pieces.

That beating shook me awake, and I started to think about what was happening to my country, to my home. Why was my father being punished? Why did people hate each other and fight one another? How could I get on with the journey of my life? No one could tell me. Everybody seemed to be going nowhere.

One day I went into my father's study. The Red Guards had not taken his large collection of books during the ransack. I had never taken any notice of them before. Since the Cultural Revolution started, we only read Chairman Mao's book.

I stared at the books. They were locked in the bookcases, which were sealed with paper strips bearing the Red Guards' seals. I slowly took the hinges off the doors of the bookcases, carefully opening them up to keep the locks and seals intact.

Over the following months I stayed home and read almost everything that was in those bookcases. Most of the books were banned materials, especially the books by Western authors like Victor Hugo, Charles Dickens and Jack London. Day after day, I buried myself in these books. For the first time I realized there were many different kinds of people in the world — some good, some evil, some strong, some weak. Yet each one of us had to face our own destiny, pursue our own future.

One day when I was restless, I walked out into our courtyard. On all sides I could see the familiar walls of my house. Above me I could see nothing but a square of blue sky.

Suddenly I decided to climb the wall to the roof. I was amazed at the scene around me as I looked out over the roofs of Beijing. They were all covered with sturdy tiles that stretched into the distance. Some of the roofs were connected; some were not.

I started to make my way over the tiles, keeping my steps light and safe. It was slippery, and if I wasn't careful I would fall and break my neck.

I had lived around my own little courtyard for years but had never got to know the neighbors. Now I saw a pretty girl in one of the courtyards. She sat in the yard knitting, a pair of crutches by her side. In another courtyard there was a flock of pigeons. The owner looked like a retired factory worker. He had about twenty pigeons, and he called each one by name as he let them out. Later I was told that the Red Guards had tried to confiscate the old man's pigeons, but he stood in front of his gate with a meat cleaver and yelled, "Whoever dares to touch my pigeons, I'll kill him." The Red Guards finally gave up and left him alone.

This teacup shows Mao with General Lin Biao, a political rival who tried unsuccessfully to wrest power from him.

For a long time I stood on the roof alone and watched the pigeons rise
up into the sky and listened to their whistles ringing far and near.

THREE

In 1968, Chairman Mao called on all students to go to the countryside to learn how to be farmers. The scary part was that we should be prepared to stay in the countryside for the rest of our lives.

Soon a list of names and destinations was posted. I was being sent to a small village in Shanxi Province, 1000 kilometers northwest of Beijing. I was fifteen years old.

The platforms of the Beijing Railway Station were filled with families and friends saying goodbye to their loved ones. My father was still in custody, so my mother came by herself to see me off. When the train started to move, she walked toward me and said something, but her words were lost in the wave of shouting. I saw tears in her eyes, even though she was trying to smile. I watched as her face faded in the crowd and felt in that moment that I had grown up. I was going to face a strange world. I was no longer a kid.

Nine hours later, the train stopped at a small station. We loaded our luggage onto horse-drawn carts that would carry us to our different destinations. It was a cold winter night. No one spoke as we rode along. I stared out at the distant mountains, lost in the thudding of the horses hooves.

When we arrived in the village it was very dark and quiet. There was no electricity – the peasants used oil lamps and drew their water from wells.

We were shown to a house. It was warm inside, and there was a huge brick bed that seven of us would share. We had been given the best house in the village because we were from Beijing.

As we turned up the oil lamp, we were surprised to find that someone had carried in water from the well and filled the kettle. There was a bag of sunflower seeds on the table. It was a small gift, nothing special, but we felt as if we were not all alone there. Somebody was taking care of us.

The village was Da Ru Hai. About eight hundred villagers lived there.

The students were assigned to five different production teams. Our team leader was a tall, big man with solid muscles. We were told that he was a champion wrestler. The next day when we started work, he simply said to us, "Don't overdo it. You've got plenty of time ahead of you."

The first morning, the team leader and a boy called Doggie took us to the frozen lake. Our job was to cut several holes in the ice. It was something new and we began enthusiastically.

I worked with Doggie. He was sixteen, with solid muscles. I asked him why we had to cut holes in the ice. He said the villagers kept fish in the lake, and we had to make holes so the fish could have fresh air.

I was puzzled. Fish breathed underwater through gills. Why did we have to cut holes for them to breathe? But Doggie said that was what they had always done.

I began to explain the difference between the respiratory functions of humans and fish. Doggie listened without saying a word. Suddenly, he said impatiently, "Why don't you just shut up and do as you are told?" I was embarrassed, not knowing how I had offended him.

Real farm work began the next day. The team leader sent us to the field to work with the other peasants. The task was simple. We had to load soil into two baskets and carry them with a pole on our shoulders to the low-lying land not far away.

Each time I put down my empty baskets, Doggie suddenly appeared in front of me. Without a word, he began to fill my baskets until they were piled high with soil.

He straightened up and looked at me. His eyes seemed to smile.

I tested the load with my hands and felt it was not very heavy.

I started to count each trip I made. One, two, three… thirteen, fourteen… Soon I was soaked with sweat and my steps began to sway. I tried to keep up with the others, but the young village men and women

overtook me, chatting and laughing. I forgot to count the trips as I fell far behind the others.

Whenever I returned with the empty baskets, Doggie would mysteriously appear right in front of me and, quick as a flash, fill them up to the brim before I had time to take a breath. Obviously, he was expecting to have some fun at my expense. I was determined not to give him the satisfaction.

Under the thin fabric of my shirt, my skin was raw and badly bruised by the pole. The pain was unbearable whenever the pole touched my shoulder. I began to carry the weight on my neck to ease the pain. My body was bent forward like a bow, but I put on a brave show whenever I stood in front of Doggie. The villagers just smiled.

The next day was worse. My shoulders were red and swollen. I had to roll up my shirt and put it around my shoulders to ease the pain.

I braced myself to carry the heavy load. I moved a few steps forward, and then, as one foot suddenly gave way, I tripped, dropped the baskets and landed on my face in the dirt. Everybody laughed. Doggie was doubled over with mirth.

I struggled to my feet and saw that most of the contents of the baskets had spilled. I dropped the baskets at Doggie's feet. He filled them up only halfway and said, "Go on."

"Fill them all the way up," I growled. I was nearly out of my mind with rage.

Doggie hesitated, and then did as I said. Other people realized that something was wrong with me and asked me to take a break. But I just bent my head and moved forward with unsteady steps. I said to myself, "You can do it. You can do it…"

Throughout the long winter, we did the same work as the villagers from sunrise to sunset, day after day. I won the trust and friendship of Doggie.

Letters from home told me that my father had been sent to a labor camp in the south of China. He was in poor health. My mother was in a labor camp in Hebei Province. My sister had gone to work on a farm in the northeast. Later, my brother was sent to a village on the outskirts of Beijing. Grandma was in Beijing alone, looking after our home.

In my village, there were fourteen students — seven boys and seven girls. The girls were responsible for cooking. White flour was available once a week, meat and rice once a month. Our main food was corn — corn breakfast, corn lunch and corn dinner. Each person could have one bottle of cooking oil per year.

Compared with the villagers, we felt lucky to have enough food to eat. Every day, after carefully weighing the food from the storeroom, the girls closed the door with a big lock.

One day there was a quarrel. After dinner, my friend Zhu began to play an accordion. He started to sing a song we used to sing when we were kids. It was about rowing a little boat on the lake.

The girls emerged from the kitchen and scolded us. "Shut up. That is not a revolutionary song." Everyone was offended. We all joined Zhu and started to sing even more loudly.

"Stop, stop!" the girls shouted, but no one was listening. They left the room and slammed the door behind them, while we kept singing and laughing.

Country life was tough for the girls. They had to do the same work as we did. They had to push wheelbarrows full of stones along a narrow bridge and carry huge bundles of corn stalks up a hill. They learned how to live with only one bath a month.

Sometimes we went to the lake to swim after work. The villagers never swam there because they were afraid of cold water.

One hot summer evening, we all went swimming. When we jumped into the water, we could feel waves spread across the lake. We were so happy, especially the girls. They were laughing and splashing. After digging in the field all day in the summer heat, the cold water felt wonderful.

Suddenly, the girls stopped laughing. When I turned around, I was stunned to see a crowd of villagers standing on the dam. There were men, women, old people and children. They all stared at us silently.

We tried to make conversation. "Come in for a swim! It's fun. Come on in!"

Nobody replied. More and more spectators gathered on the dam, just staring at us. The girls started to hide their bodies under the water, even though they wore bathing suits.

It was a long time before somebody broke the silence. A granny accompanied by her daughters pointed at the girls with her stick.

"Look at their skin, fine like silk."

"Yes," one of her daughters added. "City girls do look different from us." Then everybody began to discuss the differences between country girls and city girls.

It began to get dark. The poor girls stayed under the water. Finally they managed to swim to the other side of the lake, where they waited for us to bring their clothes.

Two years passed. Every day was the same. We got used to the hard work and coarse food, but life in the village became very boring.

I was seventeen years old. I had not been to school for four years, and I realized I would probably never go back.

One day, I asked Doggie what he wanted to do with his life. He said he had grown up in a home where nine people lived under the same roof. Now he wanted to build a small house for himself and have a family of his own. That was his dream.

But what was my dream? I was hungry to learn, but had no idea what more I could learn in this village. There was no radio, no newspapers. We had no idea what was going on outside the village.

I had brought two books with me, hidden in my suitcase — *Les Misérables* by Victor Hugo, and *War and Peace* by Tolstoy. When I came home exhausted from working in the fields, I would sit under the flickering light and read. Suddenly I was in Paris or in Moscow with the characters

in those books. I found myself living in two worlds — the real world, pale and dreary, and the book world, which was full of emotion and colors.

But no matter how much joy the books gave me, in the morning I would wake up and follow the others to the field.

Occasionally, during the break, I lay on the ground and looked up at the blue sky while my mind wandered. What was I going to do with my life? Then a loud voice would call, "Hey! Get up. Back to work." And I would walk back to the field and laugh at myself. I was a farmer.

Zhu was one of my best friends. He was a funny guy, full of energy, and he often had some surprising ideas.

One day he said he had something to show me. He opened a small wooden box. There were colorful tubes in it.

"Look," he said, "I got these from my mother's drawer. They're oil paints."

We went to the lake and sat down. I looked at the scene in front of me. The evening sky was gold. The water in the lake looked cool, clear and blue. A waterwheel, farm houses and the mountains were reflected in the distance. I saw all kinds of colors and shades.

Suddenly I couldn't wait to mix the paint, to put my colors on paper. I forgot everything around me.

Much later, I heard Zhu behind me. "Hey," he said. "You're a real artist."

Looking at the painting I had just completed, I was filled with happiness. I had found my own path at last, the path that would allow me to express myself as a human being. I might be a farmer, but I could also be myself.

That evening, I wrote to my father and told him I wanted to be an artist.

I remembered a painting I had seen in one of my father's art books. Under the vast stormy sky lay a dark landscape. There were no trees, no houses. Just a winding road that led into the endless distance.

I felt as if I was in that painting, and I was following that road to a place full of color, beauty, joy and kindness.

In a large public arena in Beijing, in 1977, my father read a new poem celebrating the end of the Cultural Revolution.

EPILOGUE

Ange lived in the village of Da Ru Hai for three years before moving to Hubei Province. There he worked in a pencil factory, operating the machine that puts the foil cylinders on pencils. During the seven long years he spent there, he continued to work on his art.

By 1976, Mao was dead, and the Cultural Revolution was over. Ange's father's reputation was restored. Ange moved back to the family home in Beijing and applied to the Central Academy of Drama to study stage design and art. He graduated with honors in 1982 and started to work as a professional stage designer at the Chinese National Opera Theater.

Today Ange lives in Toronto, Canada, where he is a successful artist and illustrator.

(Above) One of my early paintings.

(Below) In Tiananmen Square during the Cultural Revolution. Behind me are revolutionary posters.

CHINA'S CULTURAL REVOLUTION

念念不忘阶级斗争！ 横扫一切牛鬼蛇神！

敌人不投降 就叫它灭亡！

群丑图

China, a vast country containing one-fifth of the world's population, has been rich in literature, art, philosophy and medicine since ancient times. But the country also has a long history of oppression. For nearly five thousand years a small, privileged class of corrupt landlords ruled the poor farmers and peasants who made up more than 80 percent of the population.

At different times groups of people rebelled to improve their lives. But such rebellions were put down. In 1949, Mao Zedong and the Chinese Communist Party overthrew the existing regime and created the People's Republic of China. Mao set about to completely transform the entire country. He wanted to take land from the landlords and distribute

This cartoon, first printed in a Red Guard tabloid, was an important work of art in the early years of the Cultural Revolution. It shows caricatures of a number of high-ranking leaders accused of belonging to an anti-Communist Party group.

it to the people. He wanted to bring all business and industry under the control of the state. His reforms were drastic and sudden and led to great confusion, but he pushed ahead.

In 1966 Mao decided that his revolution had not gone far enough. People's thinking had not changed. So he launched the next phase of reform — the Cultural Revolution. Mao wanted to get rid of China's old ideas, old customs, old culture and old habits and replace them with new, better ones.

MAO ZEDONG

Mao Zedong was born in 1893. He belonged to a fairly well-to-do farming family led by a hot-tempered, strict father who hated to see his children idle and often beat them. Mao began working in the fields when he was six. Though Chinese children were taught to revere and obey their parents, Mao was unusually strong-willed and independent. When he was thirteen, his father humiliated him in front of guests, calling him lazy and useless. Mao swore at him and left the house. His father ran after him and ordered him to return. Mao stood at the edge of a pond and threatened to jump in if his father came nearer. He finally apologized only when his father agreed not to beat him. It was a life-changing moment for Mao. He learned that giving in only led to further oppression, and that open rebellion was the only way to stand up for his rights.

Mao left school to work on the land when he was thirteen, but at seventeen he returned to his studies, reading everything he could get his hands on — newspapers, the biographies of George Washington and Napoleon, the European philosophers. He joined the army for a time, then continued to read and study and worked as a teacher. In 1921 he helped to found the Chinese Communist Party, becoming its leader in 1935.

Postcards and posters of Mao were very popular during the Cultural Revolution.

In 1949 Mao took the Communist Party to power, establishing the People's Republic of China and becoming its Chairman. Though he constantly battled critics within his own party, to the Chinese people he remained the undisputed leader of the country until his death in 1976: "If Chairman Mao says it is so, then it is so, and if he says it is not so, then surely it is not so."

The old ideas, he said, were held by the bad "blacks" — property owners, intellectuals, writers, artists, factory owners, and even officials, or cadres, of the Communist Party who were using their position to gain special privileges. The new ideas were held by the good "reds" — the peasants, workers and members of the army.

The Red Guards

Mao saw young people as the future of his revolution.

They were loyal, brave, energetic and idealistic. They would join together to build a new China where selfless, hard-working citizens put aside their individual needs for the good of the group.

Mao encouraged students to question the wisdom of their teachers, principals and the cadres. "To rebel is justified!" he said, and millions of teenagers took up the call by organizing groups called Red Guards (*Hong Wei Bing*). Soon every school had a Red Guard detachment. Huge rallies were held, each one bigger than the last. At one rally, six thousand open trucks packed with Red Guards paraded before Mao. Tiananmen Square was filled with students, all wearing buttons with Mao's picture, waving copies of his Little Red Book and chanting, "Chairman Mao is our supreme commander and we are his little soldiers."

Everyone wanted to join the Red Guards to show that they were true revolutionaries. In this early phase of the revolution to be a Red Guard, you had to be one of the "good guys" — a child of a worker, peasant or soldier. The Red Guards rounded up the "bad guys," including teachers, artists and writers. They forced them to wear tall cardboard dunce caps and big signs around their necks. They led them around on all fours in front of jeering crowds. Some of the "enemies" were put in prison or sent to camps to do manual labor. Others were beaten to death. Many could not stand the harassment and committed suicide.

The head of a work group is forced to wear a dunce cap. Written on the cap are the crimes he has been accused of – following capitalist thinking and opposing the revolution.

Schools and universities were closed so young people could devote all their time to making revolution. They made huge posters and plastered them everywhere. They dressed in army uniforms with thick leather belts and bright red armbands. They paraded through the streets carrying banners, beating drums, gongs and cymbals, waving Mao's Little Red Book and shouting, "Long live Chairman Mao! Long Live the Cultural Revolution!"

Even small children called themselves the Chairman's Little Red Guards. They memorized passages from the Little Red Book even before they knew how to read. They set up stands on street corners where people could rest while the children recited Mao's works and served tea. They formed street-cleaning brigades to help the cause.

For young people, it was an exciting time, like a huge street party. There was no schoolwork – just lots of time to gather with friends, meet fellow Red Guards, have vigorous discussions about Mao's thoughts and how his teachings could best be put into action. They sang revolutionary songs and marched down the streets in huge packs. Loudspeakers blared from the early hours of the morning. No one slept. The young people had power. They were changing the world.

Spreading the Word

China was soon filled with nearly 100 million Red Guards. Most were young people. At first they were students who were free from school, on the loose and full of energy. The government encouraged Red Guard groups to take the message of the revolution around the country. They would spread Mao's word and at the same time meet other Red Guard groups, see how people lived in the countryside, get to know one another and understand what it meant to be

MAO'S LITTLE RED BOOK

The Little Red Book was a small, plastic-covered volume containing 420 quotations from Chairman Mao. It was the bible of the Cultural Revolution, and hundreds of millions of copies were published.

The book described the Maoist virtues of courage, thrift and devotion, and told people how to apply these values to their political work and their daily lives. Reading and learning Mao's teachings word by word brought the 800 million Chinese together and gave them a common language. They memorized the sayings and chanted them together in great throngs, like a national anthem. Though 80 percent of the people could not read before the revolution, the Little Red Book spurred people to learn. Young people taught illiterate elders how to read the book, character by character, sentence by sentence. Some memorized all 88,000 words.

In this poster students with their Little Red Books proclaim, "We must learn from our highest director. We must carry out his wishes faithfully, truthfully and courageously."

members of society where everyone was the same, everyone was equal.

Red Guards could get free train tickets, meals for ten cents, free accommodation in empty schools and stadiums. When the trains became overcrowded, many traveled on foot, walking hundreds of miles from village to village while the government provided pamphlets on how to handle blisters and frostbite. Some pushed wheelbarrows filled with pamphlets and

Mao's badges. At each stop they would bang drums, hand out their wares and spread Mao's message.

The Red Guards also spread Mao's message through millions of Big Character Posters (*dazibao*). The posters were as big as doors. They were pasted on every wall and fence, hung from clotheslines, plastered on floors and pavements and dangled from balconies, rooftops and window ledges.

Young students parade through the streets of Harbin wearing Red Guard armbands and carrying red-tasseled spears to celebrate National Day.

Trouble in the Red Guards

The Red Guards took up Mao's cause with gusto. But anyone could put on an army tunic, buy a red armband and make up a Red Guard unit. Instead of spreading Mao's ideas and being good examples, Red Guard groups began to fight against each other, as each group claimed to be the true soldiers of Mao.

China was soon in chaos. Many of the people who ran the country had been kicked out of office. Food was scarce and the transportation system was overloaded, packed with Red Guards roaming the countryside, sleeping in train stations, gathering in the streets. Schools, theaters, clubs and sports facilities had been shut down. For many young people, there was little to do but hang out and look for trouble.

Trouble came by the end of 1966. Some Red Guard groups stole weapons and equipment from the army. Others put on helmets and attacked one another with homemade bombs, slings, spears, and sticks.

Some thought that being a good revolutionary meant beating up the bad people with leather belts, raiding their homes, spitting on them. Red Guards went out into the streets, smashing road signs and lights. They broke into schools, museums, libraries and private homes and destroyed or burned anything considered old or foreign — antiques, family albums, musical instruments, paintings, religious artifacts, books by Western authors. They defaced temples, gravestones and monuments — painting over carvings and paintings in the Summer Palace in Beijing, and hacking up the Statue of Liberty in Guangzhou.

The Red Guards wore pants and shirts made from plain cloth, either blue or khaki. Anyone who wore other clothes could be stopped and their pants could even be ripped up the seams. Red Guards cut off girls' braids, shaved the heads of landlords. Shops were forced to stop selling "frivolous" items such as makeup, games or jazz records. Hairdressers were told not to give perms. Stores selling fashionable items like high heels, pointed-toed shoes or fur coats had their signs torn down and were told to display only Mao's

These boys belonging to the Little Red Guards walked 240 miles (400 km) and waited overnight in front of a bookstore to buy the new edition of *The Selected Works of Mao Zedong* and *Quotations from Mao Zedong*.

picture or slogans in their shop windows. Red Guard groups changed the names of buildings, shops and streets. Some even changed their own names.

It was an exhausting, confusing and frightening time. Some young people became tired and bored and drifted back to school. Others began to question the fighting, when they saw how the Red Guards had smashed things up everywhere.

The Move to the Country

Mao ordered the Red Guards to disband in the summer of 1968. Some went back to school; others were sent to the countryside. Families were split up. Millions of young people, born and raised in cities and towns, were told to leave their homes for good and settle in small villages. They would learn from the peasants, the peasants would learn from them, and the differences between town and country, the educated and illiterate, would be eliminated. The former Red Guards would now build Mao's new China by doing farm work. The program was called *Shang-shan xia-xiang* — "up to the mountains and down to the villages."

China's agricultural system was very primitive, and the biggest need was to create more farmland. Swamps had to be filled in, fields plowed, irrigation ditches dug. There was no big machinery and too few draft animals, so people did all the work, pulling carts and pushing wheelbarrows. Earth, stones and manure were moved in wooden buckets or round wicker baskets slung from the ends of shoulder poles.

The work was hard. Many of the teenagers had never done manual labor before. They worked long days, often in blistering heat, harvesting rice and wheat with sickles, planting trees and orchards, hacking hollows out of the rocky hillside and filling them with soil, moving boulders, hoeing cornfields, carving cisterns out of rock to collect rainwater.

When they were not working in the fields, the "city youths" would read newspapers, tell revolutionary stories and sing revolutionary songs to the villagers. In the evenings they would all study the works of Chairman Mao together.

The peasants did not always welcome the newcomers with open arms. They sometimes found them to be lazy, poor workers who didn't even know how to hold a hoe. And many of the city teens resented their time in the country, too. The work was tedious and boring. The accommodation was spare and there was no privacy. Several young people might sleep in a bare room on a bed made from a cement slab. They missed their families. They watched as their years of schooling slipped away.

Some of the young people spent the rest of their lives in the country. Some, homesick and weary, sneaked back to the cities, or even made their way south to try swimming the five miles (8 km) to Hong Kong.

Others spent several years of their youth farming or working in factories before they returned to the cities. Most never returned to school, and became adults with the equivalent of a sixth grade education. Between 1968 and 1976, 14 million young people, mostly former Red Guards, were sent to the countryside.

The End of the Cultural Revolution

By 1976, with Mao's death, the Cultural Revolution had come to an end. The "bad" people were released from prison, the schools reopened and people slowly began to rebuild their lives. Soon after Mao's death, his opponents came to power.

ARTISTS DURING THE CULTURAL REVOLUTION

By insisting that anything old or foreign was "bad," the Cultural Revolution tossed onto the trash heap thousands of years of culture — both China's own rich heritage, and all of European art, literature and philosophy. During the Cultural Revolution, theaters and museums were closed. Only works that served the revolution — poems, songs, ballets — were performed again and again (and people flocked to see them). All art that had no political usefulness, such as landscape art, was considered trivial. Paintings, ballets, films, music or books that did not serve the revolution were called "poisonous weeds" that must be uprooted and killed. The only good art was art that was created by a group or with the approval of the group, such as large murals or billboards showing revolutionary themes, used to decorate public buildings. The creators of these works were paid as a factory worker or farmer might be paid, with any profit going to the people's state.

A newspaper cartoon protests against the renowned Chinese artist Qi Baishi, saying, "Down with Qi Baishi, the black model of reactionary artists."

55

Photographs on pages 1 and 2: With my father and my mother in Beijing.
Below: Taking part in a life drawing class in a village in 1980. I am on the left, wearing glasses.

Text and illustrations copyright © 2004 by Ange Zhang
First paperback edition 2019

Groundwood Books / House of Anansi Press
groundwoodbooks.com

 Canada Council for the Arts Conseil des Arts du Canada

 ONTARIO ARTS COUNCIL
CONSEIL DES ARTS DE L'ONTARIO
an Ontario government agency
un organisme du gouvernement de l'Ontario

With the participation of the Government of Canada
Avec la participation du gouvernement du Canada | Canadä

We gratefully acknowledge for their financial support of our publishing program the Canada Council for the Arts, the Ontario Arts Council and the Government of Canada.

 FSC
MIX
Paper from responsible sources
FSC® C012700

Library and Archives Canada Cataloguing in Publication
Zhang, Ange, author
Red land, Yellow River : a story from the Cultural Revolution / Ange Zhang. — Paperback edition.
Previously published: Toronto : Groundwood Books, 2004.
ISBN 978-1-77306-270-9 (softcover)
1. Zhang, Ange—Childhood and youth. 2. China—History—Cultural Revolution, 1966-1976—Personal narratives—Juvenile literature. I. Title.
DS778.7.Z46 2019   j951.05'6092   C2018-906308-4

The illustrations were done digitally in Painter.
Design by Michael Solomon
Printed and bound in Malaysia

CREDITS AND ACKNOWLEDGMENTS
All images courtesy of the author except for the following: page 49 artist Weng Ruolan and page 55 published by the editorial office of the *Jinggang Mountain Fighting Report* / Morris & Helen Belkin Art Gallery; pages 51, 53 and 54 copyright © Li Zhensheng (Contact Press Images); page 52 Janek Rowinski Collection, Hoover Institution on War, Revolution and Peace, Stanford University.
The author and publishers would like to thank Victor Falkenheim.